Step-by-Step, Practical Recipes Curries

Fish & Seafood

Fish is really great in curries. Its short cooking time also means you can put together a meal really quickly.

Poultry & Meat

A curry is everyone's favourite dish. The ones below make quick, easy to prepare chicken, lamb, beef and pork dishes.

Vegetables

Vegetable curries are common in Indian cooking, and are a really great way for vegetarians to enjoy tasty meals.

FLAME TREE has been creating family-friendly, classic and beginner recipes for our bestselling cookbooks for over 20 years now. Our mission is to offer you a wide range of expert-tested dishes, while providing clear images of the final dish so that you can match it to your own results. We hope you enjoy this super selection of recipes – there are plenty more to try! Titles in this series include:

Cupcakes • Slow Cooker • Curries Soups & Starters • Baking & Breads Cooking on a Budget • Winter Warmers Party Cakes • Meat Eats • Party Food Chocolate • Sweet Treats

www.flametreepublishing.com

Fish & Okra Curry

INGREDIENTS

Serves 4–6

few saffron strands

450 g/1 lb fish fillets, such as
   haddock or salmon

2 tbsp vegetable oil

1 tsp fenugreek seeds

1 tsp cumin seeds

small piece cinnamon stick, bruised

4 green cardamom pods, cracked

2 garlic cloves, peeled and chopped

1 medium onion, peeled and chopped

1 tsp ground coriander

1 tsp chilli powder

4 medium tomatoes, chopped

300 ml/½ pint vegetable or
   fish stock

225 g/8 oz okra, trimmed and
   sliced diagonally

freshly ground black pepper

lemon wedges, to garnish

warm Indian-style bread, to serve

1 Place the saffron strands in a small bowl and cover with hot but not boiling water. Leave for at least 10 minutes. Skin the fish fillets, if necessary, and remove any pin bones. Cut into small chunks and reserve.

2 Heat the oil in a large frying pan, add the seeds and cook for 30 seconds, or until they pop. Add the cinnamon stick and cardamom pods and cook for 30 seconds before adding the garlic, onion, ground coriander and chilli powder.

3 Cook for 2 minutes, stirring, then add the chopped tomatoes and stock. Bring to the boil, then reduce the heat and simmer for 10 minutes.

4 Add the fish to the pan with the okra and continue to cook for 5–8 minutes, or until the fish is tender and the okra is cooked. Add black pepper to taste. Serve garnished with the lemon wedges and warm bread.

2

3

4

Red Prawn Curry with Jasmine-scented rice

INGREDIENTS

Serves 4

½ tbsp coriander seeds

1 tsp cumin seeds

1 tsp black peppercorns

½ tsp salt

1–2 dried red chillies

2 shallots, peeled and chopped

3–4 garlic cloves

2.5 cm/1 inch piece fresh galangal or
   root ginger, peeled and chopped

1 kaffir lime leaf or 1 tsp kaffir lime rind

½ tsp red chilli powder

½ tbsp shrimp paste

1–1½ lemon grass stalks, outer leaves
   removed and thinly sliced

750 ml/1¼ pints coconut milk

1 red chilli deseeded and thinly sliced

2 tbsp Thai fish sauce

2 tsp soft brown sugar

1 red pepper, deseeded and
   thinly sliced

550 g/1¼ lb large peeled tiger prawns

2 fresh lime leaves, shredded

2 tbsp fresh mint leaves, shredded

2 tbsp Thai or Italian basil leaves,
   shredded

freshly cooked Thai fragrant rice,
   to serve

1 Using a pestle and mortar or a spice grinder, grind the coriander and cumin seeds, peppercorns and salt to a fine powder. Add the dried chillies one at a time and grind to a fine powder.

2 Place the shallots, garlic, galangal or ginger, kaffir lime leaf or rind, chilli powder and shrimp paste in a food processor. Add the ground spices and process until a thick paste forms. Scrape down the bowl once or twice, adding a few drops of water if the mixture is too thick and not forming a paste. Stir in the lemon grass.

3 Transfer the paste to a large wok and cook over a medium heat for 2–3 minutes or until fragrant.

4 Stir in the coconut milk, bring to the boil, then lower the heat and simmer for about 10 minutes. Add the chilli, fish sauce, sugar and red pepper and simmer for 15 minutes.

5 Stir in the prawns and cook for 5 minutes, or until the prawns are pink and tender. Stir in the shredded herbs, heat for a further minute and serve immediately with the cooked rice.

1

2

4

Malaysian Fish Curry

INGREDIENTS

Serves 4-6

4 firm fish fillets, such as salmon, haddock or pollack, each about 150 g/5 oz in weight

1 tbsp groundnut oil

2 garlic cloves, peeled and crushed

2.5 cm/1 inch piece fresh root ginger, peeled and grated

1 tsp turmeric

1 tsp ground coriander

2 tbsp Madras curry paste

300 ml/½ pint coconut milk

2 tbsp freshly chopped coriander

lime wedges, to garnish (optional)

stir-fried Oriental vegetables and fragrant rice, to serve

1 Preheat the oven to 180°C/350°F/Gas Mark 4. Lightly rinse the fish fillets and pat dry with absorbent kitchen paper. Place in a lightly oiled ovenproof dish.

2 Heat the oil in a frying pan, add the garlic and ginger and fry for 2 minutes. Add the turmeric, ground coriander and curry paste and cook for a further 3 minutes, stirring frequently. Take off the heat and gradually stir in the coconut milk. Cool slightly then pour over the fish.

3 Cover with lightly buttered foil and cook in the preheated oven for 20 minutes, or until the fish is tender. Sprinkle with chopped coriander then garnish with lime wedges, if using, and serve with stir-fried vegetables and freshly cooked rice.

1

2

3

Seafood in Green Curry Sauce

INGREDIENTS

Serves 4

175 g/6 oz cod or haddock
  fillet, skinned

175 g/6 oz salmon fillet, skinned

225 g/8 oz monkfish fillet, skinned

1 tbsp vegetable oil

1 small onion, peeled and chopped

small piece fresh root ginger, peeled
  and grated

2 lemon grass stalks, crushed and
  outer leaves discarded

3 kaffir lime leaves

1 Thai red chilli, deseeded
  and chopped

1 tbsp Thai green curry paste,
  or to taste

1 tbsp light soy sauce

300 ml/'/₂ pint coconut milk

120 ml/4 fl oz water

2 tbsp lime juice

2 tbsp freshly chopped coriander

freshly cooked fragrant rice, to serve

1 Remove any pin bones if necessary from the fish and cut into small chunks; reserve.

2 Heat the oil in a wok or large saucepan, add the onion and fry for 2 minutes, stirring frequently. Add the ginger, lemon grass, lime leaves and chopped chilli and continue to stir-fry for 3 minutes.

3 Add the green curry paste and soy sauce, stir well then add the coconut milk and water. Bring to the boil, then reduce the heat and simmer for 5 minutes.

4 Add the fish and continue to simmer for 12–15 minutes, or until the fish is cooked. Add the lime juice, stir in the chopped coriander and serve with the freshly cooked fragrant rice.

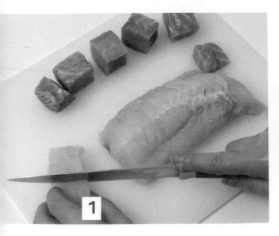

1

2

4

Thai Coconut Crab Curry

INGREDIENTS

Serves 4-6

1 onion
4 garlic cloves
5 cm/2 inch piece fresh root ginger
2 tbsp vegetable oil
2–3 tsp hot curry paste
400 g/14 oz coconut milk
2 large dressed crabs, white and
  dark meat separated
2 lemon grass stalks, peeled
  and bruised
6 spring onions, trimmed
  and chopped
2 tbsp freshly shredded Thai basil or
  mint, plus extra, to garnish
freshly boiled rice, to serve

1 Peel the onion and chop finely. Peel the garlic cloves, then either crush or finely chop. Peel the ginger and either grate coarsely or cut into very thin shreds. Reserve.

2 Heat a wok or large frying pan, add the oil and when hot, add the onion, garlic and ginger and stir-fry for 2 minutes, or until the onion is beginning to soften. Stir in the curry paste and stir-fry for 1 minute.

3 Stir the coconut milk into the vegetable mixture with the dark crabmeat. Add the lemon grass, then bring the mixture slowly to the boil, stirring frequently.

4 Add the spring onions and simmer gently for 15 minutes or until the sauce has thickened. Remove and discard the lemon grass stalks.

5 Add the white crabmeat and the shredded basil or mint and stir very gently for 1–2 minutes or until heated through and piping hot. Try to prevent the crabmeat from breaking up.

6 Spoon the curry over boiled rice on warmed individual plates, sprinkle with basil or mint leaves and serve immediately.

Aromatic Seafood Curry

INGREDIENTS

Serves 4-6

few saffron strands
450 g/1 lb assorted seafood, such as
  prawns, mussels, squid, scallops
  and white fish fillets
2 tbsp groundnut oil
4 green cardamom pods, cracked
2 whole star anise
3 garlic cloves, peeled and crushed
1 bird's eye chilli, deseeded
  and chopped
2 lemon grass stalks, bruised and
  outer leaves discarded
5 cm/2 inch piece fresh root ginger,
  peeled and grated
1–2 tbsp curry paste, or to taste
300 ml/½ pint coconut milk
150 ml/¼ pint water
1 tbsp rice wine
4 spring onions, trimmed and shredded
freshly cooked Thai fragrant rice,
  to serve

1 Cover the saffron strands in cooled boiled water and leave to soak for at least 10 minutes. Prepare the seafood, cleaning the prawns and discarding the thin black vein, if necessary. Scrub the mussels, discarding any that do not close. Rinse the squid and cut into strips, remove the vein from the scallops and cut in half, if large. Cut the fish fillets into small strips. Reserve.

2 Heat the oil in a large saucepan, add the cardamom pods, star anise, garlic, chilli, lemon grass and ginger and gently fry for 1 minute. Stir in the curry paste and cook for 2 minutes.

3 Take off the heat and gradually stir in the coconut milk and water. Bring to the boil, then reduce the heat and simmer for 5 minutes.

4 Add the seafood, starting with the fish pieces, and cook for 2 minutes. Add the prawns, mussels and scallops and cook for a further 3 minutes. Add the squid with the rice wine and cook for 2–3 minutes, or until all the fish is tender. Spoon into a warmed serving dish, sprinkle with the spring onions and serve with fragrant rice.

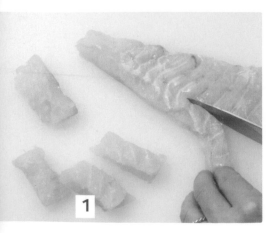

1

2

4

Green Chicken Curry

INGREDIENTS

Serves 4

1 onion, peeled and chopped

3 lemon grass stalks, outer leaves
  discarded and finely sliced

2 garlic cloves, peeled and
  finely chopped

1 tbsp freshly grated root ginger

3 green chillies

zest and juice of 1 lime

2 tbsp groundnut oil

2 tbsp Thai fish sauce

6 tbsp freshly chopped coriander

6 tbsp freshly chopped basil

450 g/1 lb skinless, boneless chicken
  breasts, cut into strips

125 g /4 oz fine green beans, trimmed

400 ml can coconut milk

fresh basil leaves, to garnish

freshly cooked rice, to serve

1 Place the onion, lemon grass, garlic, ginger, chillies, lime zest and juice, 1 tablespoon of groundnut oil, the fish sauce, coriander and basil in a food processor. Blend to form a smooth paste, which should be of a spoonable consistency. If the sauce looks too thick, add a little water. Remove and reserve.

2 Heat the wok, add the remaining 1 tablespoon of oil and when hot add the chicken. Stir-fry for 2–3 minutes, until the chicken starts to colour, then add the green beans and stir-fry for a further minute. Remove the chicken and beans from the wok and reserve. Wipe the wok clean with absorbent kitchen paper.

3 Spoon the reserved green paste into the wok and heat for 1 minute. Add the coconut milk and whisk to blend. Return the chicken and beans to the wok and bring to the boil. Simmer for 5–7 minutes, or until the chicken is cooked. Sprinkle with basil leaves and serve immediately with freshly cooked rice.

TASTY TIP

Use Thai holy basil in this recipe if possible. Thai leaves are flatter and coarser with a stronger, more pronounced flavour.

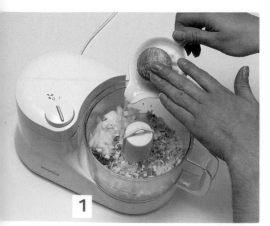

Aromatic Chicken Curry

INGREDIENTS

Serves 4

125 g/4 oz red lentils

2 tsp ground coriander

½ tsp cumin seeds

2 tsp mild curry paste

1 bay leaf

small strip of lemon rind

600 ml/1 pint chicken or
   vegetable stock

8 chicken thighs, skinned

175 g/6 oz spinach leaves, rinsed
   and shredded

1 tbsp freshly chopped coriander

2 tsp lemon juice

salt and freshly ground black pepper

To serve:

freshly cooked rice

natural yogurt

1 Put the lentils in a sieve and rinse thoroughly under cold running water.

2 Dry-fry the ground coriander and cumin seeds in a large saucepan over a low heat for about 30 seconds. Stir in the curry paste.

3 Add the lentils to the saucepan with the bay leaf and lemon rind, then pour in the stock.

4 Stir, then slowly bring to the boil. Turn down the heat, half-cover the pan with a lid and simmer gently for 5 minutes, stirring occasionally.

5 Secure the chicken thighs with cocktail sticks to keep their shape. Place in the pan and half-cover. Simmer for 15 minutes.

6 Stir in the shredded spinach and cook for a further 25 minutes or until the chicken is very tender and the sauce is thick.

7 Remove the bay leaf and lemon rind. Stir in the coriander and lemon juice, then season to taste with salt and pepper. Serve immediately with the rice and a little natural yogurt.

Persian Chicken Biryani

INGREDIENTS

Serves 4-6

2–3 tbsp vegetable oil

700 g/1½ lb boneless skinless
   chicken pieces (breast and thighs),
   cut into 2.5 cm/1 inch pieces

2 medium onions, peeled and
   coarsely chopped

2 garlic cloves, peeled and
   finely chopped

2.5 cm/1 inch piece
   ginger root, chopped

1 tsp ground turmeric

½ tsp chilli powder

1 tsp ground coriander

1 tsp ground cumin

200 g/7 oz long-grain white rice

1 tbsp tomato purée

1 tsp saffron strands

salt and freshly ground black pepper

100 ml/3½ fl oz pomegranate juice

900 ml/1½ pints chicken stock

125 g/4 oz ready-to-eat dried apricots
   or prunes, halved

2 tbsp raisins

2 tbsp freshly chopped coriander

pomegranate seeds,
   to garnish (optional)

1   Heat the oil in a large heavy-based saucepan over a medium-high heat. Cook the chicken pieces, in batches, until lightly browned. Return all the browned chicken to the saucepan.

2   Add the onions to the saucepan, reduce the heat to medium and cook for 3–5 minutes, stirring frequently, until the onions begin to soften. Add the garlic, ginger, turmeric, chilli powder, coriander, cumin and rice and stir to coat the rice.

3   Cook for about 2 minutes until the rice is golden and translucent. Stir in the tomato purée and the saffron strands, then season to taste with salt and pepper.

4   Add the pomegranate juice and stock and bring to the boil, stirring once or twice. Add the apricots or prunes and raisins and stir gently. Reduce the heat to low and cook for 30 minutes until the chicken and rice are tender and the liquid is absorbed.

5   Turn into a shallow serving dish and sprinkle with the chopped coriander. Serve immediately, garnished with pomegranate seeds, if using.

1

2

4

Red Chicken Curry

INGREDIENTS

Serves 4

225 ml/8 fl oz coconut cream

2 tbsp vegetable oil

2 garlic cloves, peeled and
   finely chopped

2 tbsp Thai red curry paste

2 tbsp Thai fish sauce

2 tsp sugar

350 g/12 oz boneless, skinless
   chicken breast, finely sliced

450 ml/³/₄ pint chicken stock

2 lime leaves, shredded

chopped red chilli, to garnish

freshly boiled rice or steamed Thai
   fragrant rice, to serve

1 Pour the coconut cream into a small saucepan and heat gently. Meanwhile, heat a wok or large frying pan and add the oil. When the oil is very hot, swirl the oil around the wok until the wok is lightly coated, then add the garlic and stir-fry for about 10–20 seconds, or until the garlic begins to brown. Add the curry paste and stir-fry for a few more seconds, then pour in the warmed coconut cream.

2 Cook the coconut cream mixture for 5 minutes, or until the cream has curdled and thickened. Stir in the fish sauce and sugar. Add the finely sliced chicken breast and cook for 3–4 minutes, or until the chicken has turned white.

3 Pour the stock into the wok, bring to the boil, then simmer for 1–2 minutes, or until the chicken is cooked through. Stir in the shredded lime leaves. Turn into a warmed serving dish, garnish with chopped red chilli and serve immediately with rice.

TASTY TIP

For a savoury-style rice, cook the rice in a light stock instead of water.

Stir-fried Chinese Chicken Curry

INGREDIENTS

Serves 4–6

350 g/12 oz skinless,
  boneless chicken
1 egg white
1 tsp salt
1 tbsp cornflour
2 tbsp groundnut oil
225 g/8 oz carrots, peeled and cut
  into very thin batons
1 large red pepper, deseeded and cut
  into thin strips
1 large green pepper, deseeded and
  cut into thin strips
1–2 tbsp curry paste
175–200 ml/6–7 fl oz chicken stock
1 tbsp rice wine or dry sherry
1 tsp demerara sugar
1 tbsp light soy sauce
6 spring onions, trimmed and
  diagonally sliced
freshly cooked sticky rice, to serve

1   Cut the chicken into small bite-sized pieces and place in a large bowl. Beat the egg white in a separate bowl until fluffy then beat in the salt and cornflour.

2   Pour over the chicken and leave to stand for 15 minutes. Heat a wok or frying pan and when hot, add the oil. Heat for 30 seconds, then drain the chicken and add to the wok or frying pan and cook, stirring, for 2–3 minutes, or until sealed.

3   Remove the chicken and reserve. Add the carrots and peppers to the wok or frying pan and cook, stirring, for 3 minutes, or until the carrots have begun to soften. Stir in the curry paste and cook, stirring, for a further 2 minutes.

4   Add the stock, rice wine or sherry, sugar and soy sauce. Stir well until blended then return the chicken to the pan with the spring onions. Cook for 3–4 minutes, or until the chicken is thoroughly cooked. Serve with the sticky rice.

1

2

3

Chicken & Chickpea Korma

INGREDIENTS

Serves 4–6

350 g/12 oz skinless,
   boneless chicken

2 tbsp vegetable oil

2 onions, peeled and cut into wedges

2–4 garlic cloves, peeled
   and chopped

2–3 tbsp Korma curry paste

1 tsp garam masala

1/2–1 tsp ground cloves

450 ml/³/₄ pint chicken stock

225 g/8 oz ripe tomatoes, peeled and
   chopped

400 g/14 oz can chickpeas, drained
   and rinsed

4 tbsp double cream

6 spring onions, trimmed and
   diagonally sliced

Indian-style bread, to serve

1 Cut the chicken into small strips and reserve. Heat the oil in a wok or frying pan, add the chicken and cook, stirring, for 3 minutes, or until sealed. Remove and reserve.

2 Add the onion and garlic to the pan and fry gently for 5 minutes, or until the onion has begun to soften. Add the curry paste, garam masala and ground cloves and cook, stirring, for 2 minutes. Return the chicken to the pan and stir well.

3 Add the stock, tomatoes and chickpeas, then bring to the boil, reduce and simmer for 15–20 minutes, or until the chicken is cooked. Stir in the cream. Spoon into a warmed serving dish, sprinkle with the spring onions and serve with Indian-style bread.

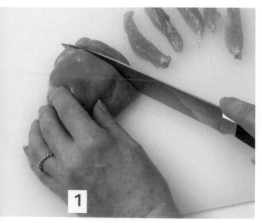
1

1

3

Beef & Mushroom Curry

INGREDIENTS

Serves 4

700 g/1½ lb rump steak

3 tbsp vegetable oil

2 onions, peeled and thinly sliced
   into rings

2 garlic cloves, crushed

2.5cm/1 inch piece ginger
   root, chopped

2 fresh green chillies, deseeded
   and chopped

1½ tbsp medium curry paste

1 tsp ground coriander

350g/12oz long-grain rice

60g/2oz butter

225g/8oz button mushrooms,
   wiped and sliced

900 ml/1½ pints beef stock

3 tomatoes, chopped

salt and freshly ground black pepper

60g/2oz creamed coconut, chopped

2 tbsp ground almonds

TASTY TIP

Finely slice 5 or 6 fresh green chillies and fry them briefly in olive oil, to make a spicy relish for those who like their curries extra hot.

1 Beat the steak until very thin, then trim off and discard the fat and cut into thin strips. Heat the oil in a saucepan, add the beef and fry until sealed, stirring frequently. Remove beef and place to one side.

2 Fry the onions, garlic, ginger, chillies, curry paste and coriander for 2 minutes. Add the mushrooms, stock and tomatoes and season to taste.

3 Return the beef to the pan. Cover the pan and simmer gently for 1¼ – 1½ hours or until the beef is tender.

4 Place the rice in a saucepan of boiling salted water, and simmer for 15 minutes until tender or according to the package directions. Drain the rice then return to the saucepan, add the butter, cover and keep warm.

5 Stir the creamed coconut and ground almonds into the curry, cover the pan and cook gently for 3 minutes. Serve with the rice.

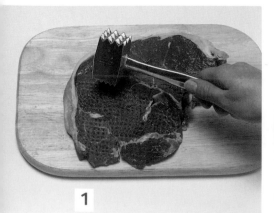
1

3

4

Beef Curry with Lemon & Arborio Rice

INGREDIENTS

Serves 4

450 g/1 lb beef fillet

1 tbsp olive oil

2 tbsp green curry paste

1 green pepper, deseeded and cut
into strips

1 red pepper, deseeded and cut
into strips

1 celery stick, trimmed and sliced

juice of 1 fresh lemon

2 tsp Thai fish sauce

2 tsp demerara sugar

225 g/8 oz Arborio rice

15 g/ ½ oz butter

2 tbsp freshly chopped coriander

4 tbsp crème fraîche

1 Trim the beef fillet, discarding any fat, then cut across the grain into thin slices. Heat a wok, add the oil and when hot, add the green curry paste and cook for 30 seconds. Add the beef strips and stir-fry for 3–4 minutes.

2 Add the sliced peppers and the celery and continue to stir-fry for 2 minutes. Add the lemon juice, Thai fish sauce and sugar and cook for a further 3–4 minutes, or until the beef is tender and cooked to personal preference.

3 Meanwhile, cook the Arborio rice in a saucepan of lightly salted boiling water for 15–20 minutes, or until tender. Drain, rinse with boiling water and drain again.

4 Return to the saucepan and add the butter. Cover and allow the butter to melt before turning it out onto a large serving dish. Sprinkle the cooked curry with the chopped coriander and serve immediately with the rice and crème fraîche.

TASTY TIP

Try using lime juice instead of lemon for an equally aromatic but less sharp flavour.

1

2

4

Spicy Pork

INGREDIENTS

Serves 4

4 tbsp groundnut oil

2.5 cm/1 inch piece fresh root ginger,
   peeled and cut into matchsticks

1 garlic clove, peeled and chopped

2 medium carrots, peeled and cut
   into matchsticks

1 medium aubergine, trimmed
   and cubed

700 g/1½ lb pork fillet, thickly sliced

400 ml/14 fl oz coconut milk

2 tbsp Thai red curry paste

4 tbsp Thai fish sauce

2 tsp caster sugar

227 g can bamboo shoots in brine,
   drained and cut into matchsticks

salt, to taste

lime zest, to garnish

freshly cooked rice, to serve

1 Heat a wok or large frying pan, add 2 tablespoons of the oil and when hot, add the ginger, garlic, carrots and aubergine and stir-fry for 3 minutes. Using a slotted spoon, transfer to a plate and keep warm.

2 Add the remaining oil to the wok, heat until smoking, then add the pork and stir-fry for 5–8 minutes or until browned all over. Transfer to a plate and keep warm. Wipe the wok clean.

3 Pour half the coconut milk into the wok, stir in the red curry paste and bring to the boil. Boil rapidly for 4 minutes, stirring occasionally, or until the sauce is reduced by half.

4 Add the fish sauce and sugar to the wok and bring back to the boil. Return the pork and vegetables to the wok with the bamboo shoots. Return to the boil, then simmer for 4 minutes.

5 Stir in the remaining coconut milk and season to taste with salt. Simmer for 2 minutes or until heated through. Garnish with lime zest and serve immediately with rice.

TASTY TIP

To balance the creamy taste of the coconut milk, squeeze the juice of half a lime into the dish and stir well, just before serving.

Lamb Korma

INGREDIENTS

Serves 4

1 tsp hot chilli powder

1 tsp ground cinnamon

1 tsp medium hot curry powder

1 tsp ground cumin

salt and freshly ground black pepper

2 tbsp groundnut oil

450 g/1 lb lamb fillet, trimmed

4 cardamom pods, bruised

4 whole cloves

1 onion, peeled and finely sliced

2 garlic cloves, peeled and crushed

2.5 cm/1 inch piece fresh root ginger,
  peeled and grated

150 ml/¼ pint Greek yogurt

1 tbsp freshly chopped coriander

2 spring onions, trimmed and
  finely sliced

To serve:

freshly cooked rice

naan bread

1 Blend the chilli powder, cinnamon, curry powder, cumin and seasoning with 2 tablespoons of the oil in a bowl and reserve.

2 Cut the lamb fillet into thin strips, add to the spice and oil mixture and stir until coated thoroughly. Cover and leave to marinate in the refrigerator for at least 30 minutes.

3 Heat the wok, then pour in the remaining oil. When hot, add the cardamom pods and cloves and stir-fry for 10 seconds. Add the onion, garlic and ginger to the wok and stir fry for 3–4 minutes until softened.

4 Add the lamb with the marinading ingredients and stir-fry for a further 3 minutes until cooked. Pour in the yogurt, stir thoroughly and heat until piping hot.

5 Sprinkle with the chopped coriander and sliced spring onions then serve immediately with freshly cooked rice and naan bread.

Lamb Pilaf

INGREDIENTS

Serves 4

2 tbsp vegetable oil

25 g/1 oz flaked or slivered almonds

1 medium onion, peeled and
finely chopped

1 medium carrot, peeled and
finely chopped

1 celery stalk, trimmed and
finely chopped

350 g/12 oz lean lamb,
cut into chunks

¼ tsp ground cinnamon

¼ tsp chilli flakes

2 large tomatoes, skinned,
deseeded and chopped

grated rind of 1 orange

350 g/12 oz easy-cook brown
basmati rice

600 ml/1 pint vegetable or lamb stock

2 tbsp freshly snipped chives

3 tbsp freshly chopped coriander

salt and freshly ground black pepper

To garnish:

lemon slices

sprigs of fresh coriander

1 Preheat the oven to 140°C/275°F/Gas Mark 1. Heat the oil in a flameproof casserole dish with a tight-fitting lid and add the almonds. Cook for about 1 minute until just starting to brown, stirring often. Add the onion, carrot and celery and cook gently for a further 8–10 minutes until soft and lightly browned.

2 Increase the heat and add the lamb. Cook for a further 5 minutes until the lamb has changed colour. Add the ground cinnamon and chilli flakes and stir briefly before adding the tomatoes and orange rind.

3 Stir and add the rice, then the stock. Bring slowly to the boil and cover tightly. Transfer to the preheated oven and cook for 30–35 minutes until the rice is tender and the stock is absorbed.

4 Remove from the oven and leave to stand for 5 minutes before stirring in the chives and coriander. Season to taste with salt and pepper. Garnish with the lemon slices and sprigs of fresh coriander and serve immediately.

1

2

4

Goan-style Beef Curry

INGREDIENTS

Serves 4–6

2 onions, peeled and chopped

2–3 garlic cloves, peeled
  and chopped

5 cm/2 inch piece fresh root ginger,
  peeled and grated

1 tsp chilli powder

1 tsp turmeric

1 tsp ground coriander

1 tsp ground cumin

freshly milled salt

450 g/1 lb braising steak, trimmed

2 tbsp vegetable oil

2 green chillies, deseeded and cut in
  half lengthways

2 red chillies, deseeded and cut in
  half lengthways

450 ml/³/₄ pint beef stock

1 Place the onions, garlic, ginger and spices in a food processor and blend to a paste.

2 Spread half the paste half over the steak, then sprinkle lightly with salt. Leave to marinate in the refrigerator for at least 15 minutes.

3 Cut the beef into small strips. Heat 1 tablespoon of the oil in a heavy-based saucepan, add the beef and fry on all sides for 5 minutes, or until sealed. Remove from the pan and reserve.

4 Add the remaining oil to the pan, then add the halved chillies and fry for 2 minutes. Remove and reserve. Stir the remaining paste into the oil left in the pan and cook for a further 3 minutes. Return the beef to the pan with the beef stock and bring to the boil.

5 Reduce the heat, cover and simmer for 30–40 minutes, or until tender. Garnish with the halved chillies and serve.

1

2

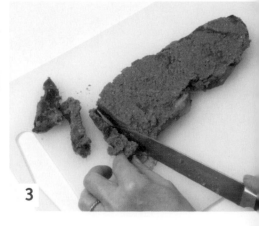

3

Thai-style Cauliflower & Potato Curry

INGREDIENTS

Serves 4

450 g/1 lb new potatoes, peeled and
    halved or quartered
350 g/12 oz cauliflower florets
3 garlic cloves, peeled and crushed
1 onion, peeled and finely chopped
40 g/1½ oz ground almonds
1 tsp ground coriander
½ tsp ground cumin
½ tsp turmeric
3 tbsp groundnut oil
salt and freshly ground black pepper
50 g/2 oz creamed coconut, broken
    into small pieces
200 ml/7 fl oz vegetable stock
1 tbsp mango chutney
sprigs of fresh coriander, to garnish
freshly cooked long-grain rice, to serve

1 Bring a saucepan of lightly salted water to the boil, add the potatoes and cook for 15 minutes or until just tender. Drain and leave to cool. Boil the cauliflower for 2 minutes, then drain and refresh under cold running water. Drain again and reserve.

2 Meanwhile, blend the garlic, onion, ground almonds and spices with 2 tablespoons of the oil and salt and pepper to taste in a food processor until a smooth paste is formed. Heat a wok, add the remaining oil and when hot, add the spice paste and cook for 3–4 minutes, stirring continuously.

3 Dissolve the creamed coconut in 6 tablespoons of boiling water and add to the wok. Pour in the stock, cook for 2–3 minutes, then stir in the cooked potatoes and cauliflower.

4 Stir in the mango chutney and heat through for 3–4 minutes or until piping hot. Tip into a warmed serving dish, garnish with sprigs of fresh coriander and serve immediately with freshly cooked rice.

TASTY TIP

If you want to add some colour to the dish, try replacing some of the cauliflower with broccoli florets.

2

3

3

Creamy Vegetable Korma

INGREDIENTS

Serves 4-6

2 tbsp ghee or vegetable oil
1 large onion, peeled and chopped
2 garlic cloves, peeled and crushed
2.5 cm/1 inch piece of root ginger,
   peeled and grated
4 cardamom pods
2 tsp ground coriander
1 tsp ground cumin
1 tsp ground turmeric
finely grated rind and juice of ½ lemon
50 g/2 oz ground almonds
400 ml/14 fl oz vegetable stock
450 g/1 lb potatoes, peeled and diced
450 g/1 lb mixed vegetables, such as
   cauliflower, carrots and turnip, cut
   into chunks
150 ml/¼ pint double cream
3 tbsp freshly chopped coriander
salt and freshly ground black pepper
naan bread, to serve

1 Heat the ghee or oil in a large saucepan. Add the onion and cook for 5 minutes. Stir in the garlic and ginger and cook for a further 5 minutes, or until soft and just beginning to colour.

2 Stir in the cardamom, ground coriander, cumin and turmeric. Continue cooking over a low heat for 1 minute, stirring.

3 Stir in the lemon rind and juice and almonds. Blend in the vegetable stock. Slowly bring to the boil, stirring occasionally.

4 Add the potatoes and vegetables. Bring back to the boil, then reduce the heat, cover and simmer for 35–40 minutes, or until the vegetables are just tender. Check after 25 minutes and add a little more stock if needed.

5 Slowly stir in the cream and chopped coriander. Season to taste with salt and pepper. Cook very gently until heated through, but do not boil. Serve immediately with naan bread.

Vegetable Kofta Curry

INGREDIENTS

Serves 6

350 g/12 oz potatoes, peeled
and diced

225 g/8 oz carrots, peeled and
roughly chopped

225 g/8 oz parsnips, peeled and
roughly chopped

1 medium egg, lightly beaten

75 g/3 oz plain flour, sifted

8 tbsp sunflower oil

2 onions, peeled and sliced

2 garlic cloves, peeled and crushed

2.5 cm/1 inch piece fresh root ginger,
peeled and grated

2 tbsp garam masala

2 tbsp tomato paste

300 ml/½ pint vegetable stock

250 ml/9 fl oz Greek yogurt

3 tbsp freshly chopped coriander

salt and freshly ground black pepper

TASTY TIP

Leaving the cooked, drained vegetables to go completely cold before puréeing will result in a nice firm batter, without too much liquid in it.

1 Bring a saucepan of lightly salted water to the boil. Add the potatoes, carrots and parsnips. Cover and simmer for 12–15 minutes, or until the vegetables are tender. Drain the vegetables and mash until very smooth. Stir the egg into the vegetable purée, then add the flour and mix to make a stiff paste and reserve.

2 Heat 2 tablespoons of the oil in a wok and gently cook the onions for 10 minutes. Add the garlic and ginger and cook for a further 2–3 minutes, or until very soft and just beginning to colour.

3 Sprinkle the garam masala over the onions and stir in. Add the tomato paste and stock. Bring to the boil, cover and simmer gently for 15 minutes.

4 Meanwhile, heat the remaining oil in a wok or frying pan. Drop in tablespoons of vegetable batter, four or five at a time and fry, turning often, for 3–4 minutes until brown and crisp. Remove with a slotted spoon and drain on absorbent kitchen paper. Keep warm in a low oven while cooking the rest.

5 Stir the yogurt and coriander into the onion sauce. Slowly heat to boiling point and season to taste with salt and pepper. Divide the koftas between warmed serving plates and spoon over the sauce. Serve immediately.

Thai Curry with Tofu

INGREDIENTS

Serves 4

750 ml/1¼ pints coconut milk
700 g/1½ lb tofu, drained and cut
   into small cubes
salt and freshly ground black pepper
4 garlic cloves, peeled and chopped
1 large onion, peeled and cut
   into wedges
1 tsp crushed dried chillies
grated rind of 1 lemon
2.5 cm/1 inch piece fresh root ginger,
   peeled and grated
1 tbsp ground coriander
1 tsp ground cumin
1 tsp turmeric
2 tbsp light soy sauce
1 tsp cornflour
Thai fragrant rice, to serve

To garnish:

2 red chillies, deseeded and cut
into rings
1 tbsp freshly chopped coriander
lemon wedges

1 Pour 600 ml/1 pint of the coconut milk into a saucepan and bring to the boil. Add the tofu, season to taste with salt and pepper and simmer gently for 10 minutes. Using a slotted spoon, remove the tofu and place on a plate. Reserve the coconut milk.

2 Place the garlic, onion, dried chillies, lemon rind, ginger, spices and soy sauce in a blender or food processor and blend until a smooth paste is formed. Pour the remaining 150 ml/¼ pint coconut milk into a clean saucepan and whisk in the spicy paste. Cook, stirring continuously, for 15 minutes, or until the curry sauce is very thick.

3 Gradually whisk the reserved coconut milk into the curry and heat to simmering point. Add the cooked tofu and cook for 5–10 minutes. Blend the cornflour with 1 tablespoon of cold water and stir into the curry. Cook until thickened.

4 Turn into a warmed serving dish and garnish with chilli, lemon wedges and coriander. Serve immediately with Thai fragrant rice.

Creamy Chickpea Curry

INGREDIENTS

Serves 4–6

2 tbsp vegetable oil

1 cinnamon stick, bruised

3 cardamom pods, bruised

1 tsp fennel seeds

5 cm/2 inch piece fresh root ginger, peeled and grated

2 garlic cloves, peeled and crushed

2 red chillies, deseeded and chopped

1 large onion, peeled and chopped

1 tsp ground fenugreek

1 tsp garam masala

$\frac{1}{2}$ tsp turmeric

2 x 400 g/14 oz cans chickpeas, drained and rinsed

300 ml/$\frac{1}{2}$ pint water

1 tsp tomato purée

300 ml/$\frac{1}{2}$ pint coconut milk

225 g/8 oz cherry tomatoes, halved

2 tbsp freshly chopped coriander

1 Heat the oil in a frying pan, add the cinnamon stick, cardamom pods, fennel seeds and ginger and cook gently for 3 minutes, stirring frequently. Add the garlic, chillies, onion and remaining spices to the pan and cook gently, stirring occasionally, for 3–5 minutes, or until the onion has softened.

2 Add the chickpeas and water. Bring to the boil, then reduce the heat and simmer for 15 minutes.

3 Blend the tomato purée with a little of the coconut milk then add to the chickpeas with the remaining coconut milk and tomatoes. Cook for 8–10 minutes, or until the tomatoes have begun to collapse. Stir in the chopped coriander and serve.

TASTY TIP

Medium-sized tomatoes can be used, if preferred – simply chop rather than halve and use as above.

1

2

3

Step-by-Step, Practical Recipes Curries: Tips & Hints

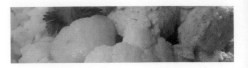

Food Fact

There are many different kinds of fresh chillies and, generally, the smaller they are the fiercer the heat. Red chillies are generally milder than green ones because they sweeten as they become riper. The tiny, slender tapering red or green bird's eye chillies are very hot and pungent. Thai cooks often include the seeds in cooking, but to moderate the heat, scrape out and discard the seeds.

Helpful Hint

Dried red chillies are used throughout Asian countries. The drying process concentrates the flavour, making them fierier. Look for dried chillies with a bright red colour and a pungent aroma. If stored in a sealed container, they will keep almost indefinitely. Chilli oil is made from crushed dried chillies or whole fresh chillies and is used as both a seasoning and a dipping condiment. Chilli powder is made from dried red chillies and is usually mixed with other spices and seasonings, ranging from mild and aromatic to very hot – always check the jar before using.

Helpful Hint

With curries it is important to remember the basic philosophy of a balance of fresh produce combined with the flavours of preserved, dried, salted and fermented ingredients. Most ingredients are now available in ordinary supermarkets and a few of the more unusual ones in Asian groceries and markets.

Food Fact

Fresh root ginger has a pungent, spicy, fresh taste. It is usually peeled, then finely chopped or grated. Vary the amount used to suit your own taste. For just a hint, slice thickly and add to the dish when cooking, then remove just before serving. Fresh ginger is infinitely preferable to the powdered variety, which loses its flavour rapidly. Fresh ginger should feel firm when you buy it. If you have more than you need, it can be used within a week. Store it in the freezer as it can be grated from frozen.

Food Fact

Tofu or bean curd has been used as an ingredient in Asian cooking for over 1,000 years. Made from yellow soya beans, which are soaked, ground and briefly cooked, tofu is rich in protein and low in calories. Because of its bland taste it is ideal cooked with stronger flavourings. It is usually available in two types: a soft variety known as silken tofu that can be used for soups and desserts, and a firm, solid white block, which can be cubed or sliced and included in stir-frying and braising. Also available is smoked tofu, which is seasoned bean curd. When using, cut into the required size with care and do not stir too much when cooking; it simply needs to be heated through.

Helpful Hint

Every curry will of course have a main ingredient such as meat, chicken, fish, seafood, vegetables or cheese. Always use the best quality ingredients that you can afford and play to their own strengths. You should try and get free range meat which has come from animals that have led happier lives and fed on pastures rather than artificial feeds. It always pays dividends to find a specialist butcher, grocer and fishmonger whom you can trust to provide good quality foodstuffs. Likewise, local farm shops can be invaluable sources.

Helpful Hint

Oil or fat is essential in curries. Without it the spices are harsher and with much less flavour and aroma. Indian restaurants tend to use ghee, which is a clarified butter, but olive oil, sunflower or groundnut oil can be used. Add plenty when starting the dish, it will separate and excess can be skimmed off at the end and kept covered in the fridge for use with your next curry.

Helpful Hint

Creamed coconut is made from coconut oils and other fats and comes in a hard, white block. It is not a substitute for coconut milk and is usually added at the end of cooking, to thicken a sauce or to add coconut flavour to a finished dish.

Tasty Tip

Fresh coriander is the most popular fresh herb used in cooking curries. It has an appearance similar to flat-leaf parsley, but has a pungent, slightly citrus flavour. Leaves, stems and roots are all used, so buy in big fresh bundles if possible.

First published in 2013 by
FLAME TREE PUBLISHING LTD
Crabtree Hall, Crabtree Lane, Fulham,
London, SW6 6TY, United Kingdom
www.flametreepublishing.com

The CIP record for this book is available from the British Library • Printed in China

NOTE: Recipes using uncooked eggs should be avoided by infants, the elderly, pregnant women and anyone suffering from an illness.

18 17 16 15 14 13   10 9 8 7 6 5 4 3 2 1

ISBN: 978-0-85775-859-0

ACKNOWLEDGEMENTS: Authors: Catherine Atkinson, Juliet Barker, Gina Steer, Vicki Smallwood, Carol Tennant, Mari Mererid Williams, Elizabeth Wolf-Cohen and Simone Wright. Photography: Colin Bowling, Paul Forrester and Stephen Brayne. Home Economists and Stylists: Jacqueline Bellefontaine, Mandy Phipps, Vicki Smallwood and Penny Stephens. Some props supplied by Barbara Stewart at Surfaces. Publisher and Creative Director: Nick Wells. Editorial: Catherine Taylor, Laura Bulbeck, Esme Chapman and Emma Chafer. Design and Production: Chris Herbert, Mike Spender and Helen Wall.